MICROWAVE *Cooking*

Berryland Books

Copyright © Berryland Books Ltd 2008

0 9 8 7 6 5 4 3

All rights reserved. No part of this publication may be reproduced, stored in a retrieval system, or transmitted, in any form or by any means, electronic, mechanical, photocopying, recording or otherwise, without written permission in accordance with the provisions of the Copyright Act 1973 (as amended). Any person or persons who do any unauthorized act in relation to this publication may be liable to criminal prosecution and civil claims for damages. Berryland Books Ltd has made every effort to make sure that the contents of this book were accurate at the time of publication. The publisher, author, and editors cannot be held liable for any errors and omissions in this publication or actions that may be taken as a consequence of using it.

Managing Editor: Richard Johnston
Author: Dr. Anita Shan
Designer: Prof. Madhu Krishna, Signet Designs, India.

Printed and bound in China
ISBN 1-84577-646-18

A catalogue record of this book is available from the British Library

NB: Recipes using uncooked eggs or meat or fish should be avoided by infants, the elderly, pregnant women and anyone suffering from an illness.

Contents

Mushroom gratin with chives

Serves 4

Ingredients

- 1¼oz (40g) streaky bacon
- ½ onion
- 16oz (500g) small button mushrooms
- ½tsp (2½ml) chopped rosemary
- 1tsp (5ml) lemon juice
- Freshly ground pepper as desired
- Salt as desired
- Fat to grease the dishes
- 5fl oz (150ml) crème fraîche
- 1 egg yolk
- 1tbsp (15ml) finely chopped chives

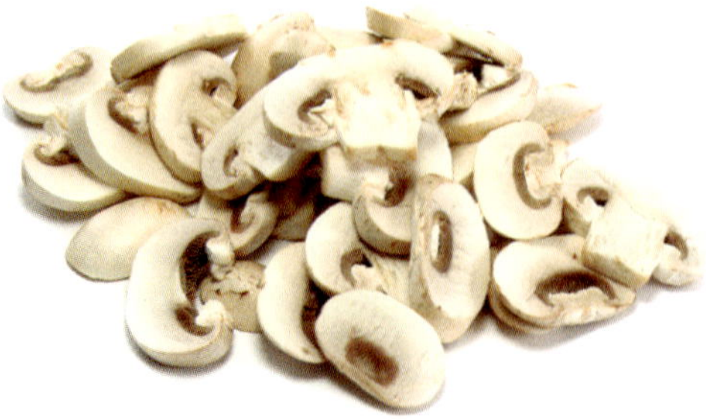

Method

1 Peel and finely dice the onion. Finely dice the bacon.

2 Clean and quarter the mushrooms.

3 Mix the bacon and onion in a microwavable dish [8¾in (22cm)], cover and cook at 600 watts for 3 minutes.

4 Mix in the mushrooms, rosemary and lemon juice, cover and cook at 600 watts for 6 minutes. Stir after 3 minutes.

5 Drain and season with salt and pepper. Divide between 4 greased fireproof dishes.

6 Mix together the crème fraîche, egg yolk and chives. Season with salt and pepper.

7 Pour the cream over the mushrooms and brown under a hot grill.

Turkey ragout with celery and tomato sauce, rice and salad

Serves 4

Ingredients

- 16oz (500g) turkey breast
- 11oz (350g) celery
- 11oz (350g) beefsteak tomatoes
- 2tbsp (30ml) vegetable oil
- Salt & freshly ground pepper as desired
- 3tbsp (45ml) red wine
- 1tbsp (15ml) cream
- 1tbsp (15ml) flour
- 2tbsp (30ml) chopped parsley

Method

1 Cut the turkey breast into strips.

2 Trim, wash and slice the celery.

3 Scald the tomatoes in boiling water for a few seconds, refresh in cold water, then skin, quarter, deseed and dice.

4 Heat a browning dish at 600 watts for 8 minutes.

5 Mix the oil with the meat and season with salt and pepper. Put into the dish. Mix in the vegetables.

6 Cover and cook at 600 watts for 16 minutes. Stir after 8 minutes.

7 Whisk together the red wine, cream and flour. Stir into the ragout and cook at 600 watts for 1 minute. Mix in the parsley and season to taste.

8 Serve with rice tossed in butter and a green salad.

Creamed potato soup with herbs

Serves 4

Ingredients

- 2 onions
- 1½oz (50g) streaky bacon
- 3½oz (100g) leeks
- 1½oz (50g) carrots
- 1½oz (50g) celery
- 8oz (250g) potatoes
- 1 bay leaf
- ¾fl oz (20ml) milk
- 16fl oz (500ml) meat stock
- 2tbsp (30ml) chopped parsley
- 1tsp (5ml) dried marjoram
- Salt & freshly ground pepper as desired
- 1 egg yolk
- 3fl oz (100ml) crème fraîche
- Nutmeg
- 1tbsp (15ml) chopped parsley

Method

1 Peel and finely dice the onions. Finely dice the bacon.

2 Clean and wash the vegetables. Cut the leeks and celery into thin strips and thinly slice the carrots. Peel, wash and thinly slice the potatoes.

3 Put the bacon and onions into a microwavable dish, cover and cook at 600 watts for 4 minutes. Stir after 2 minutes.

4 Add the vegetables, potatoes and bay leaf. Cover and cook at 600 watts for 14 minutes. Stir after 7 minutes.

5 Add the milk and stock. Add the herbs and season with salt and pepper. Cover and cook at 600 watts for 8 minutes.

6 Puree the soup in a liquidiser or with a hand blender.

7 Mix together the egg yolk and crème fraîche and stir into the soup. Heat at 600 watts for 1 minute. Add nutmeg to taste and sprinkle with parsley.

Spicy turkey curry with vegetables, cashew nuts, jelly ear fungus

Serves 4

Ingredients

- 2 Chinese mushrooms (Jelly ear fungus also known as Wood ear mushroom)
- 11oz (350g) turkey breast fillet
- 1 onion
- 2 cloves garlic
- 1 leek
- 1 red pepper
- 2 small red chillies
- 1tbsp (15ml) clarified butter
- 1tsp (5ml) freshly chopped ginger
- 1tbsp (15ml) coconut cream
- 5oz (150g) natural yoghurt
- 1tbsp (15ml) curry powder
- 1tbsp (15ml) cashew nuts
- Salt & freshly ground pepper as desired
- 2tbsp (30ml) chopped parsley

Method

1 Soak the mushrooms in hot water for ½ hour. Rinse well and cut into smaller pieces.

2 Cut the turkey breast into even 3 cm cubes. Peel and finely chop the onion and garlic. Clean the vegetables. Slice the leek at an angle and cut the pepper into strips. Chop the chillies very finely.

3 Melt the clarified butter in a large microwavable dish at 600 watts.

4 Stir in the onion, garlic and ginger. Cover with microwavable film and cook for 1 minute. Stir in the diced turkey breast, cover and cook for a further 1 minute.

5 Add the mushrooms, leek, pepper and chillies, cover and cook for 1 minute.

6 Add the coconut cream. Whisk the curry powder into the yoghurt, pour over the ingredients in the dish and mix well. Cover with the microwavable film again and cook at 600 watts for 8-10 minutes, or until done, stirring once or twice during this time.

7 Roughly chop the cashew nuts and mix into the turkey curry. Season to taste with salt and pepper. Serve sprinkled with parsley. Serve with rice.

Potatoes with peas and curry cream sauce

Serves 4

Ingredients

- 32oz (1 kg) small potatoes
- 2 onions
- ½oz (20g) butter
- 3tbsp (45ml) curry powder
- 16fl oz (500ml) vegetable stock (instant)
- 3fl oz (100ml) cream
- 8oz (250g) peas (frozen)
- Salt & freshly ground pepper

Method

1 Peel the potatoes and cut into smaller pieces if necessary. Peel and dice the onions. Put the butter and onions into a dish, cover and cook at 850 watts for about 4 minutes.

2 Add the potatoes, curry powder and stock, mix, cover and cook at 850 watts for about 10 minutes.

3 Add the cream and peas, cover and cook at 850 watts for about 10 minutes and then at 450 watts for about 5 minutes. Season with salt and pepper.

Beef and cabbage stew

Serves 4

Ingredients

- 1 onion
- 2tbsp (30ml) butter
- 6½oz (200g) beef
- 8fl oz (250ml) beef stock (instant)
- 8oz (250g) potatoes
- 8oz (250g) white cabbage
- 8oz (250g) beetroot
- 1 small leek
- 2tbsp (30ml) red wine vinegar
- Salt as desired
- 5oz (150g) crème fraîche
- 1tbsp (15ml) freshly chopped parsley

Method

1 Dice the beef. Peel and dice the onion. Peel and dice the potatoes. Shred the cabbage. Peel and grate the beetroot. Wash the leek and finely slice the white and light green parts.

2 Put the onion, butter, meat and stock into a dish, cover and cook at 850 watts for about 5 minutes. Then add the prepared vegetables with the vinegar and salt. Cook at 850 watts for about 5 minutes, then at 450 watts for about 20 minutes.

3 Stir in the crème fraîche and serve sprinkled with parsley.

Fish curry

Serves 4

Ingredients

- 12½oz (400g) pineapple (canned)
- 1 red pepper
- 1 banana
- 19oz (600g) redfish fillet
- 3tbsp (45ml) lemon juice
- 1¼oz (40g) butter
- 4fl oz (125ml) dry white wine
- 4fl oz (125ml) pineapple juice
- Salt as desired
- A pinch of sugar
- Chilli powder
- 2tbsp (30ml) curry powder
- 2tbsp (30ml) white sauce thickener

Method

1 Drain the pineapple and cut into small pieces. Wash, trim, halve and deseed the pepper, remove the white inner membranes and cut the flesh into thin strips. Cut the fish into bite-sized dice. Peel and slice the banana.

2 Put the diced fish into a dish and sprinkle with lemon juice. Add the pineapple, pepper, banana, butter, wine, juice, spices, seasonings and sauce thickener and mix well. Cover and cook at 850 watts for about 5 minutes and at 450 watts for a further 12 minutes or so.

Macaroni bake with cheese

Serves 4

Ingredients

- 9½oz (300g) macaroni
- 1oz (30g) butter
- 3 onions
- 2 red peppers
- 2 carrots
- 19oz (600g) beefsteak tomatoes
- 6½fl oz (200ml) vegetable stock (instant)
- 9½oz (300g) crème fraîche
- 5fl oz (150ml) milk
- Salt & freshly ground pepper as desired
- 1 clove garlic
- 6½oz (200g) cooked ham, diced
- 6½oz (200g) feta cheese
- 5oz (150g) Gouda cheese, grated

Method

1 Cook the macaroni in salted water until 'al dente', then drain thoroughly.

2 Peel and dice the onions.

3 Wash, trim, halve and deseed the peppers, remove the white membranes and dice the flesh.

4 Peel and slice the carrots. Wash and roughly dice the tomatoes.

5 Sauté the onions and garlic in butter until soft, add the peppers and carrots and sauté briefly, then add the stock. Mix the crème fraîche with the milk, pepper and salt, pour over the vegetables and bring to a boil briefly.

6 Put the macaroni, diced tomatoes, ham and feta cheese into a baking dish. Add the vegetable sauce and mix. Sprinkle with the grated Gouda and cook uncovered at 300 watts + 350ºF (180°C) hot air for about 30 minutes, until golden brown.

Fish fillet with green soya beans

Serves 4

Ingredients

- 4tbsp (60ml) olive oil
- Salt as desired
- Freshly ground pepper as desired
- 12½oz (400g) young fresh green soya beans
- 15 lemon balm leaves
- Juice of a lemon
- 1 clove garlic
- 4 pieces of fish fillet [each weighing about 6oz (180g)]
- 2tbsp (30ml) lemon juice
- 2 red chillies
- 8fl oz (250ml) water

Method

1 Wash the beans, put into a dish, cover and cook at 850 watts for about 5 minutes. Wash the lemon balm leaves and dry. Coarsely puree the beans (reserving a few for garnishing) and the lemon balm. Season with salt and pepper. Add 4tbsp (60ml) olive oil and lemon juice. Peel and press the garlic. Add to the mixture and mix well. Check the seasoning and add more salt and pepper if necessary.

2 Put the bean puree into a dish.

3 Wash the fish fillets, pat dry and sprinkle with lemon juice. Season with salt and pepper.

4 Wash the chillies, slit open lengthways and chop finely.

5 Place the fish in a dish and scatter the chillies on top. Add 8fl oz (250ml) water, cover and cook at 850 watts for about 7 minutes. Take out. Then cook the bean puree and the reserved beans at 850 watts for a further 1 minute. Stir well.

6 Serve the fish on the bean puree scattered with beans.

Sole rolls with crab butter

Serves 4

Ingredients

- 8 sole fillets [each weighing 3½oz (100g)]
- 2tbsp (30ml) lemon juice
- Salt & freshly ground pepper as desired
- 1oz (30g) crab butter
- 1oz (30g) flour
- 1½fl oz (50ml) white wine
- 8fl oz (250ml) water
- 1½fl oz (50ml) cream
- 3½oz (100g) shrimps
- 1 spring onion
- 2 tomatoes

Method

1 Scald the tomatoes in boiling water for a few seconds, refresh in cold water, then skin, quarter, deseed and dice finely. Wash and trim the spring onion and slice or chop.

2 Sprinkle the sole fillets with lemon juice, season with salt and pepper, roll up and place in a dish. Knead together the crab butter and the flour and add to the sole rolls in generous flakes. Mix the wine, water, cream, shrimps, spring onion and tomatoes and add to the dish. Cover and cook at 850 watts for about 8 minutes.

3 Take the fish fillets out of the dish, stir the sauce until smooth and season with salt and pepper. Pour the sauce over the sole rolls.

Pork fillet in roquefort sauce

Serves 4

Ingredients

- 16oz (500g) pork fillet
- Salt & freshly ground pepper as desired
- 3tbsp (45ml) oil
- 2 onions
- 1½fl oz (50ml) white wine
- 4fl oz (125ml) cream
- 6½oz (200g) roquefort
- 2tbsp (30ml) crème fraîche
- 2tbsp (30ml) chopped parsley

Method

1 Peel and dice the onions and put into a dish with the oil. Cover and cook at 850 watts for about 5 minutes. Add the pork fillet and turn to coat in the mixture. Add the wine, cover and cook at 450 watts for about 10 minutes.

2 Mash the Roquefort, add the cream and crème fraîche and mix smoothly. Add to the meat and mix with the wine. Cook uncovered at 450 watts for a further 5 minutes or so, stirring halfway through the cooking time.

3 To serve, slice the pork fillet, add a little sauce and sprinkle with parsley.

Chicken fillet in mustard cream

Serves 4

Ingredients

- 8oz (250g) crème fraîche
- 4tbsp (60ml) wholegrain mustard
- 1 clove garlic, crushed
- Salt as desired
- ½tsp (2½ml) sage leaves
- 4 chicken breast fillets

Method

1 Put the crème fraîche, mustard, garlic, salt and sage into a dish and mix well.

2 Coat the chicken breast fillets in the mustard cream. Cover and cook at 850 watts for about 4 minutes and then at 450 watts for about 12 minutes.

3 During this time turn the meat once and sprinkle with the mustard cream.

Cep consommé with parmesan dumplings

Serves 4

Ingredients

- 1oz (30g) dried ceps
- 16fl oz (500ml) water
- 2 onions, diced
- 26fl oz (800ml) beef stock (ready-made)
- Salt & freshly ground pepper as desired
- 3tbsp (45ml) sherry
- 1tbsp (15ml) snipped chives

For the parmesan dumplings

- 4fl oz (125ml) milk
- ½oz (15g) butter
- 1½oz (50g) semolina
- 1 small egg
- ½oz (20g) grated parmesan
- Salt as desired

Method

1 Soak the ceps in the warm water for about 15 minutes. Add the onions and the stock, cover and cook at 850 watts for about 15 minutes. Strain through a sieve and season with salt, pepper and sherry.

2 Put the milk, butter, semolina, beaten egg, parmesan and salt into a dish and mix well. Cover and cook at 850 watts for about 4 minutes, then at 150 watts for about 5 minutes, stirring occasionally.

3 Using wet teaspoons cut out small portions of the mixture and put into the hot soup. Serve sprinkled with chives.

Creamed corn soup with fried bacon

Serves 4

Ingredients

- 1 can sweetcorn [9oz (280g)]
- 1 onion, diced
- ½oz (15g) butter
- ½oz (15g) flour
- 20fl oz (600ml) vegetable stock (instant)
- 1 chilli
- Chilli powder
- Salt & freshly ground pepper as desired
- Sugar
- 3½oz (100g) cream
- 3½oz (100g) Schinkenspeck (dry-cured ham), diced

Method

1 Drain the sweetcorn. Put about ¾ of it into a bowl and add the onion, stock, chilli and seasonings. Knead together the butter and flour and add to the bowl. Cover and cook at 850 watts for about 5 minutes and then at 450 watts for about 8 minutes.

2 Puree the soup, adding the cream at the same time. Put the rest of the sweetcorn into the soup.

3 Place the diced ham in a single layer on a plate covered with kitchen paper. Then cook at 850 watts for about 3 minutes, until crisp.

4 Reheat the soup and serve sprinkled with the ham.

Cheese dumplings

Serves 4

Ingredients

- 9½oz (300g) stale white bread
- 6½fl oz (200ml) lukewarm milk
- 1 onion, diced
- 1tbsp (15ml) butter
- 5oz (150g) each of Gouda and Tilsiter cheese, coarsely grated
- 3tbsp (45ml) chopped parsley
- 2tbsp (30ml) flour
- 3 eggs
- Salt & freshly ground pepper as desired
- Approx. 3½oz (100g) browned butter

Method

1 Cut the white bread into small dice, add the milk and leave to stand for about 30 minutes.

2 Heat the butter in a pan and sauté the onion until soft. Add the onion, cheese, parsley, flour, eggs and seasonings to the bread and milk and mix well.

3 Form the mixture into 8-10 dumplings and lay them side by side in a dish. Cover with microwavable foil and cook at 600 watts for about 6 minutes and then at 450 watts for about 5 minutes.

4 Pour browned butter over the dumplings. Serve with tomato salad.

Green mashed potato with pine nuts

Serves 4

Ingredients

- 25oz (800g) potatoes (peeled weight)
- Salt & freshly ground pepper as desired
- 4tbsp (60ml) finely chopped basil
- 6½fl oz (200ml) cream
- 1tbsp (15ml) butter
- 1oz (30g) pine nuts

Method

1 Dice the potatoes, put into a dish with about 3fl oz (100ml) water and a little salt, cover and cook at 850 watts for 12-15 minutes. Drain and press through a potato ricer.

2 Puree the basil with a little of the cream, then add to the potatoes with the rest of the cream, butter and pepper and mix well.

3 Toast the pine nuts in a dry frying pan and scatter over the mashed potato.

Cucumber with dill sauce and tarragon sauce

Each serves 4

Ingredients

- 2 cucumbers (each weighing approx. 9½oz (300g))

For the dill sauce

- 3½oz (100g) crème fraîche
- 2tsp (10ml) chopped dill tips
- Salt as desired

For the tarragon sauce

- 3½oz (100g) crème fraîche
- 6½oz (200g) cream
- 6½fl oz (200ml) vegetable stock (instant)
- 2tsp (10ml) chopped tarragon leaves
- Salt & freshly ground pepper as desired

Method

1 Peel the cucumbers if necessary, then halve lengthways and scrape out the seeds with a teaspoon. Cut the cucumbers into strips or slices approximately ¼in (6mm) thick. Put into a dish, cover and cook at 850 watts for about 5 minutes.

For the dill sauce

1 Mix the crème fraîche with the dill and salt. Pour over the cooked cucumber.

For the tarragon sauce

1 Mix the crème fraîche with the cream, vegetable stock, tarragon, salt and pepper. Cook uncovered at 850 watts for about 5 minutes. Pour over the cooked cucumber.

Carrots in chervil cream

Serves 4

Ingredients

- 25oz (800g) carrots
- 1tbsp (15ml) butter
- 4fl oz (125ml) vegetable stock (instant)
- 5oz (150g) crème fraîche
- 2tbsp (30ml) white wine
- Salt & freshly ground pepper as desired
- A pinch of sugar
- 1tsp (5ml) mustard
- 3tbsp (45ml) chervil, chopped
- 1-2tbsp (15-30ml) white sauce thickener

Method

1 Peel the carrots and slice or cut into sticks. Put into a dish with the butter, stock, crème fraîche, wine, mustard, sauce thickener and seasonings and mix well. Cover and cook at 850 watts for about 6 minutes and then at 450 watts for a further 8 minutes.

Courgette cream sauce to serve with ribbon pasta

Serves 4

Ingredients

- 12½oz (400g) courgettes
- 3tbsp (45ml) olive oil
- 2 cloves garlic
- Salt & freshly ground pepper as desired
- 1tsp (5ml) dried thyme
- ½tsp (2½ml) dried rosemary
- 1½oz (50g) Gorgonzola
- 2½oz (75g) fresh cheese (e.g. cream cheese, curd cheese)
- 6½oz (200g) sour cream
- 2tbsp (30ml) chopped dill tips

Method

1 Wash and thinly slice the courgettes. Peel and finely chop the garlic. Put both into a dish with the oil, salt, pepper, thyme and rosemary, cover and cook at 850 watts for about 5 minutes.

2 Lightly mash the Gorgonzola and add to the vegetables with the fresh cheese, sour cream and dill. Mix well and cook at 850 watts for a further 5 minutes or so.

3 This sauce goes well with ribbon pasta such as tagliatelle.

Poached salmon fillet with fennel

Serves 4

Ingredients

- 4 pieces salmon fillet [each weighing 6½oz (200g)]
- 1tbsp (15ml) lemon juice
- Salt & freshly ground pepper as desired
- 1oz (30g) butter
- 1oz (30g) flour
- 1½fl oz (50ml) white wine
- 8fl oz (250ml) water
- 1½fl oz (50ml) cream
- 2 fennel bulbs

Method

1 Wash the fennel, halve lengthways and cut out the stalk. Cut the fennel into thin strips. Reserve the tender leaves.

2 Sprinkle the salmon fillets with lemon juice, season with salt and pepper and place in a dish. Knead together the butter and flour and add to the salmon in generous flakes. Add the wine, water, cream and fennel and mix. Cover and cook at 850 watts for about 8 minutes.

3 Take out the fish fillets. Stir the sauce until smooth, season with salt and pepper and stir in 1tbsp (15ml) chopped fennel leaves. Serve the fish fillets with the fennel and sauce and garnish with fennel leaves.

Lemon mousse with fruits of the forest

Serves 4

Ingredients

- 8oz (250g) yoghurt
- 1½oz (50g) crème fraîche
- Juice of 2 lemons
- 1 packet vanilla sugar
- 2½oz (80g) sugar
- 4 sheets gelatine
- 8oz (250g) cream
- 16oz (500g) mixed fruits of the forest (frozen)
- 1½oz (50g) sugar

To garnish

- Lemon balm and spirals of lemon peel

Method

1 Soak the gelatine in cold water for about 10 minutes, then squeeze out and put into the microwave at 450 watts for about 15 seconds to dissolve.

2 Mix together the yoghurt, crème fraîche, lemon juice, vanilla sugar and sugar. Mix about 2tbsp (30ml) of the yoghurt mixture with the gelatine, then stir this into the rest of the yoghurt mixture. Chill for about 3 hours.

3 When the mixture begins to set, fold in the stiffly whipped cream.

4 To serve, sprinkle the frozen fruit with sugar and thaw at 150 watts for about 10 minutes. Spoon onto dessert plates and add spoonfuls of the lemon mousse.

5 Serve garnished with lemon balm and spirals of lemon peel

Conversion guide

The Conversion guide given below is not an exact equivalent but an approximation, to make your measuring easier.

Dry Measures

Imperial	Metric
½oz	15g
1oz	30g
2oz	60g
3oz	90g
4oz (¼lb)	125g
5oz	155g
6oz	185g
7oz	220g
8oz (½lb)	250g
9oz	280g
10oz	315g
11oz	345g
12oz (¾lb)	375g
13oz	410g
14oz	440g
15oz	470g
16oz (1 lb)	500g
24oz (1½lb)	750g
32oz (2lb)	1Kg

Liquid Measures

Imperial	Metric
1fluid oz	30ml
2fluid oz	60ml
3fluid oz	100ml
4fluid oz	125ml
5fluid oz (¼pint /1gill)	150ml
6fluid oz	190ml
8fluid oz	250ml
10fluid oz (½pint)	300ml
16fluid oz	500ml
20fluid oz (1pint)	600ml
1¾pints	1000ml (1 litre)

Conversion guide

Cup & Spoon Measures

Imperial	Metric
¼tsp	1ml
½tsp	2½ml
1tsp	5ml
1tbsp	15ml
¼cup	60ml
½cup	125ml
1cup	250ml

Helpful Measures

Imperial	Metric
⅛in	3mm
¼in	6mm
½in	1cm
¾in	2cm
1in	2.5cm
2in	5cm
2½in	6cm
3in	8cm
4in	10cm
5in	13cm
6in	15cm
7in	18cm
8in	20cm
9in	23cm
10in	25cm
11in	28cm
12in	30cm

Oven temperatures

	°F (Fahrenheit)	°C (Celsius)	Gas Mark
Very low	250	120	1
Low	300	150	2
Moderately low	325	160	3
Moderate	350-375	180-190	4
Moderately hot	400-425	200-210	5
Hot	450-475	220-230	6
Very hot	500-525	240-250	7

Glossary

Al Dente In cooking, the adjective 'al dente' meaning 'to the bite' in Italian describes pasta and rice that has been cooked so as to be firm but not hard. "Al dente" describes vegetables that are cooked through but still offer resistance to the bite.

Beefsteak Tomatoes are the largest varieties of cultivated tomatoes, sometimes weighing 1 lb (½kg) or more. It is commonly used in sandwiches.

Basil The green aromatic leaves of basil or sweet basil is used fresh and dried as flavorings or spices in sauces, stews, salad dressings, vegetables, poultry, and vinegar.

Button mushrooms are young unopened mushrooms.

Celery is a cultivated plant of the parsley family with closely packed succulent leaf stalks that are eaten raw or cooked.

Chervil also called garden chervil, is a delicate annual herb, normally used to season mild-flavoured foods such as poultry, some seafoods, and young vegetables.

Crème Fraîche or fresh cream is a heavy cream slightly soured with bacterial culture, but not as sour or as thick as sour cream. It can be made at home by adding a small amount of cultured buttermilk or sour cream to normal heavy cream, and allowing to stand for several hours at room temperature until the bacterial cultures act on the cream.

Curry powder is a blend of coriander, turmeric, cumin, and fenugreek seeds. Depending on the recipe, additional ingredients such as ginger, garlic, fennel seed, clove, mustard seed, green cardamom, black cardamom, nutmeg, red pepper, cinnamon and black pepper may also be added.

Dill The fernlike leaves of Dill are aromatic, and is said to be best when used fresh, as it loses its flavor rapidly if dried.

Feta Cheese A white salty Greek cheese made from the milk of ewes or goats.

Fennel A culinary herb of the parsley family, it is grown for the dried, ripe fruits or seeds. They are widely used in Indian cuisine for their warm, sweet character.

Gorgonzola is a type of rich, strong-flavored Italian cheese with bluish-green veins.

Gouda is a flat round cheese with a yellow rind, originally made in the town of Gouda in the Netherlands.

Jelly ear fungus is conspicuously ear shaped, ranging from purple to dark brown or black in color with a rubbery texture, and most often found on dead elder trees but also on elms.

Lemon balm is a bushy herb of the mint family, with leaves smelling and tasting of lemon.

Marjoram is an aromatic undershrub with sweet pine and citrus flavor.

Nutmeg is the hard, aromatic, almost spherical seed of a tropical tree.

Parsley is used for its leaf in much the same way as coriander or cilantro, but has a milder flavor.

Pine Nuts are the edible seeds of pine trees.

Quark (Curd cheese) is a fresh cheese made from pasteurized milk. It is soft, white and unaged, similar to cream cheese.

Roquefort is a soft blue cheese made from ewes' milk. It is ripened in limestone caves and has a strong flavor.

Sage is an aromatic plant with grayish-green leaves that are used as a culinary herb, native to southern Europe and the Mediterranean.

Soyabean is a leguminous plant native to Asia, widely cultivated for its edible seeds. The fruit of this plant, used in a variety of foods and fodder, especially as a replacement for animal protein.

Tarragon is a small shrubby herb used as a basis for salad dressings. When using tarragon in cooked dishes, it is best to add it at the end, as heat tends to decrease its flavor. Unlike most of the other herbs, tarragon loses the potency of its flavor when dried. It is frequently preserved in vinegar to retain its essence.

Tilsit is a semi-hard mildly flavored cheese.